What do the CHAMELEONS do?

Series - *Children's Nature Quest*

Author
M Borhan

From
Big 6 Publishing

A Chameleon 3D Sketch

Chameleons are crucial components of their ecosystems, with unique adaptations and behaviors that contribute to biodiversity and ecosystem functioning. Their ability to change color serves not only for camouflage but also communication and thermoregulation. Predominantly insectivorous, chameleons aid in controlling insect populations, showcasing their role in ecosystem balance. Their adept climbing abilities facilitate access to various food sources and microhabitats while also aiding in evading predators. Additionally, chameleons inadvertently contribute to seed dispersal as they move through their habitats. Their sensitivity to environmental changes makes them valuable indicators of ecosystem health, with declines in populations signaling potential disturbances. Protecting chameleon populations is vital for preserving biodiversity, maintaining ecological balance, and ensuring the overall health of their habitats.

A Chameleon's Life is full of Challenges.....like-

Adaptability

Chameleons are renowned for their ability to change color, allowing them to blend into their surroundings and communicate with other chameleons.

Habitat
They inhabit a variety of ecosystems, including rainforests, deserts, and savannas, displaying a broad adaptability to different environments.

Diet
Chameleons primarily feed on insects and sometimes small vertebrates. Their long, extendable tongues aid in capturing prey from a distance.

But they have remarkable strengths too!

For Example, -

Eyesight

Possessing highly developed eyesight, chameleons can independently move each eye, providing them with a wide field of vision and aiding in hunting.

Feet Structure
Their zygodactylous feet (fused toes in opposing pairs) enable a firm grip on branches and enhance their climbing abilities

Prehensile Tail

Many chameleon species have a prehensile tail, helping them maintain balance while navigating through trees and bushes.

Size Ranges
Chameleons vary greatly in size, with some species as small as a few centimeters, while others can reach lengths exceeding half a meter.

Respiration

Chameleons possess specialized lungs that allow for efficient gas exchange, facilitating their survival in various environments.

Camouflage Abilities

Chameleons possess remarkable camouflage abilities, allowing them to blend seamlessly into their surroundings by changing their skin color and pattern. This remarkable adaptation not only helps them evade predators but also enables them to ambush prey with unparalleled stealth, showcasing their extraordinary hunting prowess in the animal kingdom.

Communication

Besides changing color for camouflage, chameleons use color displays to communicate with each other, indicating mood, territory, and mating readiness.

Thermoregulation

Their ability to change color also aids in thermoregulation, helping them regulate body temperature in different environmental conditions.

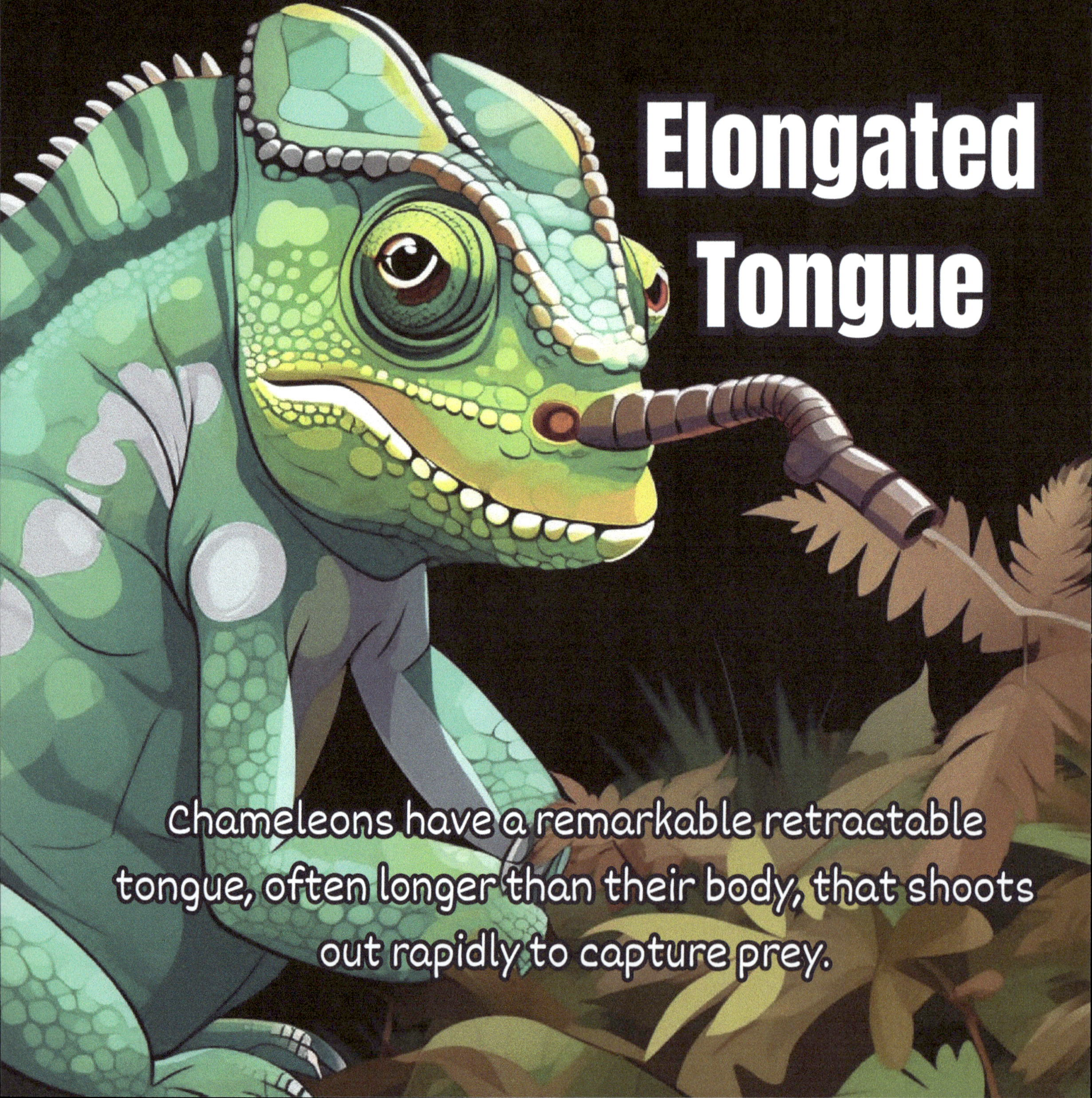

Elongated Tongue
Chameleons have a remarkable retractable tongue, often longer than their body, that shoots out rapidly to capture prey.

Slow Movement

Generally, chameleons move slowly, relying on stealth rather than speed to approach prey and avoid predators.

Nocturnal and Diurnal Habits

Chameleon species exhibit both diurnal (active during the day) and nocturnal (active during the night) behavior, depending on their habitat and species.

Mimicry
Some chameleons can mimic the appearance of leaves or other elements in their surroundings, providing them with an added layer of camouflage.

Some other remarkble features make them special too, like-
Solitary Behavior
Many chameleons are solitary creatures, coming together primarily for mating purposes.

Egg-Laying

Most chameleons are oviparous, laying eggs in concealed locations to protect them from predators.

Longevity
The lifespan of chameleons varies by species, with some living only a few months, while others can survive for several years.

Distinctive Crests

Certain chameleon species have distinctive crests or casques on their heads, which may play a role in species recognition or mating displays.

Vocalizations

While not as vocal as some other reptiles, chameleons can produce hisses or other sounds to communicate with conspecifics or deter potential threats.

So, Chameleons deserve more attention!
Biodiversity Preservation
Chameleons have a minimal ecological footprint, preserving biodiversity is possible by avoiding habitat destruction and minimizing the impact on local woods' environment.

Conservation Challenges

Chameleons face threats from habitat loss, climate change, and the exotic pet trade, making some species vulnerable or endangered. Conservation efforts are crucial to preserving their biodiversity.

www.ingramcontent.com/pod-product-compliance
Lightning Source LLC
Chambersburg PA
CBHW040201110726
48005CB00018B/2850